A Healthy Church

What It Looks Like and How to Get There From Here

Joe McKeever

Parson's Porch Books

www.parsonsporchbooks.com

A Healthy Church

ISBN: Softcover 978-1-951472-12-2

Copyright © 2019 by Joe McKeever

All rights reserved. No part of this book may be reproduced or transmitted in any form or by any means, electronic or mechanical, including photocopying, recording, or by any information storage and retrieval system, without permission in writing from the publisher.

A Healthy Church

Contents

INTRODUCTION 9

CHAPTER ONE 15
   How to Spot A Healthy Church 15
   In 30 Seconds 15

CHAPTER TWO 21
   When to Start the Conversation on Church Health 21

CHAPTER THREE 24
   Ten Signs You May Be Part of An Unhealthy Church 24

CHAPTER FOUR 32
   The Romans 12 Blueprint for Christ's Church

CHAPTER FIVE 40
   Scripture Provides A Snapshot of a 12Healthy Church
   (Acts 6:1-7) 40

CHAPTER SIX 45
   Nothing Tells the Story About A Church's Health Like Its
   Leadership 45

CHAPTER ONE 53
   What to Do with The Problem of Immature Church
   Members 53

CHAPTER TWO 58
   Let's Face It. Some Church People Hang On To Their Jobs
   Too Long. In Most Cases, It's Unhealthy. 58

CHAPTER THREE 65
  A Healthy Church Will Welcome Newcomers!
CHAPTER FOUR 73
  In A Healthy Church, Leaders Will Be People of Courage!
CHAPTER FIVE 80
  What to Do When Church Members Insist on Their Rights.. 80
CHAPTER SIX 85
  20 Steps Toward Awakening A Sleeping Church and Stirring It to Action 85
CHAPTER SEVEN 95
  What People Want from The Pastor and Have A Right to Expect 95
CHAPTER EIGHT 102
  What We Wish for The Lord's Church............................ 102
ABOUT THE AUTHOR 107

Dedication:

I'm grateful for these who made church such a pleasant experience during my early years:

--Eunice Martin taught the "card class" for preschoolers at New Oak Grove Free Will Baptist Church, Nauvoo, AL.

--Bill Montgomery taught teenagers in Sunday School, same church.

--Bill Dempsey taught college students in Sunday School at Birmingham's West End Baptist Church.

--West End's ministers contributed immeasurably to my spiritual growth as a young adult: John L. Smith, Bill Burkett, Ron Palmer, Larry Andrews. I am forever in their debt.

--Bob Ford, pastor advisor to the Birmingham-Baptist Youth Rally, which provided invaluable experience in worship planning, working with a team, leadership.

INTRODUCTION

"We can't do that. We're too small." "We'll have to leave that for the big boys." "We can't afford it." "Hey--remember where we are now."

Unbelief sometimes comes disguised as "real world thinking."

God's people walk by faith.

It's His plan from the beginning. (see Habakkuk 2:4)

Let the pastors lead and preach and serve by faith. Let them show God's people how to believe in a mighty God and be used of Him for extraordinary things.

Let the church be strong and healthy.

The vitality of a church is directly related to the obedience and faithfulness of both leadership and laity. The opening line from the Song of Deborah is a keeper: *That the leaders led in Israel, and that the people volunteered, O bless the Lord!* (Judges 5:2). When the leaders are leading and the people are doing their jobs, the work gets done, the enemy is routed, and the Lord is honored.

I am the product of a big church that grew healthy and effective in time to welcome this 19-year-old college student into its loving embrace. I flourished in that sweet fellowship. After being baptized into the membership, I met my wife-to-be, a high school senior at the time, and grew in the Lord by giant strides. Eventually I was called into the ministry, married, and ordained there.

I am honored to be part of the lasting legacy of Birmingham, Alabama's West End Baptist Church.

Alas, that wonderful vitality and warm fellowship did not last. A few years after Margaret and I married and had left to pastor a church, the leadership began squabbling among themselves. The congregation displayed its ugly side to the world in business meetings that would have made Jerry Springer proud. Not long afterwards, the church began the decline that would eventually put them out of business.

So, while that congregation taught me about sweet fellowship, healthy worship and strong ministries, they also left a lasting example of bad health, all of them lessons which linger to this day.

The Lord has a lot of 19-year-old searchers stumbling around out there, who would love to come upon a welcoming congregation that will receive them and show them the love of Christ.

"Father, help Your churches to get this right."

A Healthy Church

Part One

What the Healthy Church Looks Like

In this section, we dive right in and talk about church health, what it is and what it is not.

In Part Two, we come at the subject from various angles. The subject is huge and the books dealing with church health would fill a library. These chapters were lifted from our website because they seemed to offer helpful counsel to leaders wanting to bless the Lord's church. We tweaked them a little, but there is no particular order to the chapters.

CHAPTER ONE

How to Spot A Healthy Church In 30 Seconds

Something about those children intrigued me, but I couldn't figure out what it was.

For several weeks during my daily walk on the Mississippi River levee, I had been noticing three small children playing in their yard which joined the green expanse of the levee.

They seemed unusually happy and physically active, which the pastor/grandfather in me found charming.

The oldest child might have been seven or eight. There was a younger brother and a little sister. The yard held all kinds of play equipment.

No matter how cold it was, they were out there laughing and running, jumping and hiding, having a big time.

You could hear them a block away. They were always enjoying themselves and seemed to love one another.

"Whatever the parents are doing," I thought, "it's working."

Then, one day, I noticed something different. Another kid had joined them, and they had several large-wheel vehicles on top of the levee which they were riding down into the yard. Two women sat near the house, keeping an eye on them. One was the mother, I assumed.

As I drew closer, the children coasted off the levee, all except the oldest boy. He looked up at me and said, "Hi. I'm Harley." I was so taken aback, I had to ask, "That's your name?" It was.

I said, "Hi Harley. My name is Mister Joe." He gave a big grin and said, "Hi, Mister Joe!" Then, off the levee he went.

I walked away thinking my first impression of that family was correct. The parents were doing many things right. Here is a little kid with a great attitude, confident enough to look adults in the eye and to introduce himself.

A few days afterwards, my curiosity got the best of me. I walked off the levee and introduced myself to the adults in the yard. It turned out they were grandparents, caring for the little ones in the daytime while the parents worked. Yes, they owned a television, but no cable. No computer games. They didn't care for movies.

The kids just wanted to play.

I affirmed the grandparents on the terrific job they were doing, wished them well, and went on my way.

And that started me thinking about healthy churches.

I wondered...

Is it possible to visit a church and within a few seconds determine that it's healthy?

I ran that question by a number of friends.

Some said it's easier to tell an *unhealthy* church in a few seconds than a healthy one.

One pastor said, "If the building is in a state of disrepair and the people are unfriendly, those are dead giveaways. If there are no greeters for the church and no helps for first-time visitors, you decide very quickly this must be an unhealthy church."

Other signs are so obvious they require little comment: a sparse crowd, lackluster singing, uninspired sermons, and unfriendly congregations.

But the question persists: Can you tell a church is healthy in just a few seconds?

College Minister Corey Olivier gave several possibilities. "You notice if the people are excited to be there. That works for me."

"Also, if the people are generous, that's a great sign. Not necessarily rich. The people of Macedonia were generous but dirt-poor (Second Corinthians 8)."

"If there is strong pastoral leadership if everyone is in the right place in serving. Those are great signs. It's what I call a 'good Ephesians 4' model."

"If the people love their ministerial staff and follow them, they are going to be a healthy church in most cases."

Pastor Mike Miller said, "I need a little more than 30 seconds to determine if a church is healthy. I want to hear their preaching and learn what the preacher is telling the people theologically."

Here are more answers from friends. At the end I'll give you mine.

–people are friendly and speak to strangers.

–there's evidence of mission involvement and evangelism.

–there's an air of expectancy.

–the church has children.

–people are carrying their Bibles.

–warmth.

–a variety of age groups.

–in the parking lot and at the front door, servants are showing me Jesus in their very actions.

And my answer to the question...

If I could choose one moment, a sliver of time that would tell the story on a church and allow me to decide on the health of that congregation, it would be: How they handle a conflict.

How they deal with a problem.

Yes, healthy churches can have problems. But they have great skills in dealing with them, which sets them apart from the typical congregation.

For years, like most of us I imagine, I saw Acts 6:1-7 as the origin of the first deacons in the church. One day it hit me that that is only a minor part of that story. The thrust of that story is how the church dealt with a challenge to its fellowship and peace.

Dissension arose in the Jerusalem congregation when some minority widows began complaining that they were being neglected in the daily distribution of food in favor of the majority. While the church considered the problem and began to deal with it, people throughout the city kept an eye on that situation. Would this bunch of Christ-followers be ripped asunder by conflict? Would they show themselves to be all too human and abandon their high-minded purposes in order to fight and bicker?

Were these Christians like the rest of the world?

The community watched and was most impressed by what happened.

So. What exactly did they see?

They saw the leadership--the Apostles--move quickly when the dissent broke out. They saw the leaders and the congregation work in harmony to address the matter.

They saw the congregation do something totally unexpected: They selected some good people from the minority--the complainers! --and put them in charge of the food project.

The townspeople saw how it all worked out, how it pleased everyone and how the congregation settled back down in harmony to resume their ministry.

That's when many in the community decided.

They wanted to know more. They wanted what these Christians had.

Acts 6:7 reads, "So the preaching about God flourished, the number of disciples in Jerusalem multiplied greatly, and a large group of priests became obedient to the faith."

Question: When was the last time your church impressed the outside world by the way it dealt with conflict?

When was the last time newcomers walked into a spirited business meeting at your church and were so impressed, that within one minute they were ready to sign on the dotted line? What could they possibly have seen that would have brought about that kind of reaction?

I do not have all the answers on this. However, this would be a great subject for a discussion with your church leadership.

And that's the next chapter.

CHAPTER TWO

When to Start the Conversation on Church Health

The time to begin talking about church health with the congregational leadership is when things are going great.

Someone may insist that you are "going to stir up things" by asking them to discuss problem-solving within the congregation.

Quite the opposite. You are trying to head off problems.

One thing we know is that problems will come. Church growth may create some conflicts. Sometimes members feel they are not being heard or that leadership is being unfair. At other times, troublemakers may arrive from the outside with plans to disrupt the fellowship, divert the church from its mission, and destroy the ministry of God's servants.

Expect the trouble. Watch for problems. Have a plan.

Don't be blind-sided.

A healthy church will give advance thought on how to deal with problems when they arise.

Pastor Rick was serving a church not far from where I live. One Sunday, a man with a reputation as a troublemaker joined their fellowship.

"We didn't find out until later that the man had tried to tear up several churches. So, I quietly informed our deacon leadership and we agreed to keep an eye on him.

"Sure enough, after a few months, that guy phoned a deacon to ask if they could meet. As they sat at the table chatting, the fellow abruptly said, 'So--what are we going to do about Pastor Rick?' The deacon was ready. 'We're going to love him! Isn't he terrific?'

"That was the end of the conversation. Pretty soon that fellow was gone, and we never saw him again."

They had been prepared.

A healthy church will try to head off trouble before it gets started. Like white corpuscles flowing to an infection, key leaders rush to the scene of the trouble and deal with it.

A healthy church will have people in place and on the alert, always watching for the first sign of trouble.

One more thing about the chapters that follow. Since much of this came from my blog originally, there is some repetition in it, some scriptures used more than once, some works cited a couple of times. I decided to leave these in, since each chapter should be able to stand on its own. (I'm going to assume most people read books the way I do--a chapter or two today, another chapter next week, and so forth. So, we will not assume that those reading chapter eight, for instance, will have the points of chapter four in mind.)

I once inserted a small card in the Sunday worship bulletin to ask, "Do you have a question about how things are done around here? A problem? A criticism? Please let us know. Then, drop the card in the offering plate."

The chairman of deacons said, "Pastor, you sure you want to do that? You're going to stir up dissent." I assured good friend Mike Skiles that the opposite was the case. "If people are unhappy, they're going to talk about it. And I'd rather they say it to me so we can do something about it."

What I found was that the very act of giving people a means of voicing their questions or criticism lessened the complaints. It was a nice discovery.

I wish for you a healthy church.

CHAPTER THREE

Ten Signs You May Be Part of An Unhealthy Church

When an online magazine posted an article on "Five signs you're part of an unhealthy church," I eagerly opened it. The subject is dear to my heart.

The author's points were good, as far as they went. No argument.

A church is unhealthy when...

--1) Leadership has no clear vision.

--2) Leadership can never be challenged.

--3) You are comfortable but never challenged.

--4) Members are content with being pew warmers.

--5) Outreach is never planned or preached.

All of these are valid. But there is so much more.

Eventually, with a little help from my friends--where would I be without them! --we came up with 10 additional symptoms that a church may be unhealthy....

1. Prayer, if offered at all, is a formality, an afterthought, a burden.

I've known churches to go through an entire service without the first prayer.

While spending a long weekend with a group of pastors and their wives at a retreat in Southern Italy, I was struck by the prominence of prayer in their gathering. By the time I rose to speak, the service–by then a half-hour long–had experienced at least five prayers. Each prayer had been spontaneous, heartfelt, and a joy. I knew then we were in for a rich time of Christian fellowship.

There is no more reliable indicator of a Christian's spirituality or a congregation's health than the vitality of our prayer life. The church that can worship effectively without praying is attempting something never done in the history of Christianity.

2. Giving stems from duty and is never a joy.

We hear people say, "God is going to get it one way or the other. So you might as well give a tithe."

I don't think He wants it that way.

When David was receiving the offering for the temple, he was impressed by the generous spirit of the givers. "Then the people rejoiced for they had offered willingly, because with a loyal heart they had offered willingly to the Lord, and King David also rejoiced greatly" (I Chronicles 29:9).

…. not grudgingly or of necessity, for God loves a cheerful giver. (II Cor. 9:7)

3. Laughter is rare, and when present at all, forced and quickly stifled.

Laughter seems an embarrassment to the unhealthy church, as though they must not show themselves as normal and human.

Someone asked my friend, "Do you think Jesus ever laughed? The Bible doesn't say He did." He answered, "I don't know whether Jesus laughed or not. But He sure fixed me up so I could!"

Christians are "fixed up to laugh." Joy is the very atmosphere of the Throne room of Heaven (Psalm 16:11). It is "the business of Heaven," said C. S. Lewis. "The fruit of the Spirit is love, joy...." (Galatians 5:22).

Someone has said, "Joy is the flag flown from the castle of your heart to show the King is in residence."

"You have put gladness in my heart, more than when their grain and new wine increased" (Psalm 4:7).

4. When the service ends, everyone scatters.

There is no fellowship in an unhealthy family.

I said to a pastor where I had just preached, "Close your eyes and listen. That's the sound of fellowship." By then, the service had been over a full half-hour. But his people had hung around, visiting with one another. No one wanted to leave.

There are few greater compliments to give a church than that the members love each other and cannot wait to get together. "By this all men will know you are my disciples," our Lord said, "that you love one another" (John 13:34-35).

5. When a leader calls for volunteers, he gets few responses.

The members demand to be catered to--"That's what we pay them for!"--but find excuses to stay away when asked to serve. "I don't have a gift for that."

Leaders may try to lead, but if no one comes after them, they're only taking a walk. A great church must have strong leaders of courage and vision, commitment and strength, as well as volunteers who will go the second mile, who do more than is asked, who don't mind exerting themselves for the success of the work and the glory of the Lord.

The congregation that is forced to rely on the same few overworked volunteers is on life-support.

6. When conflict arises, leaders ignore it, panic, or jump ship.

A sick church will go to one extreme or the other: it will panic at any conflict, thinking this may be the final death-stroke, or like a sick person who experiences one illness after another, they will ignore it altogether.

George Bullard has written a book and holds conferences with the intriguing title, "Every church needs a little conflict."

A healthy church may have regular growing pains and will often be targeted by the enemy, and therefore will need to be prepared to deal with problems from inside and out.

7. The leaders have a poor understanding of Scripture.

A working knowledge of God's Word is like the underpinning of a house; it may not be the first thing you notice, but everything about the dwelling will be influenced by the foundation.

My mother, now in Heaven, went to church all her life. However, no one ever taught her how to study God's Word. She loved her Bible, read it constantly and marked it up, I'm happy to report. But one day she told me, "I just let it fall open and read there. It always seems to work out."

One has to wonder how it would have been if decades earlier, some faithful pastor had gathered the members of our rural Baptist church and taught them how to read God's Word and understand it. What if the pastor had taken the time to teach members the grand sweep of Scripture, so they understood the differences in the Old and New Testaments' doctrine, the message of the gospels and epistles, and where the various epistles fit in the larger framework.

I suspect that our pastors did not do that because they didn't know how. Being untaught themselves, they knew only certain scriptures and never ventured far from them.

Pity the church with leaders who do not know God's Word.

8. Jesus is rarely mentioned. It's all about "God."

Those who know the Word cannot get around the prominence Jesus Christ receives throughout. Scripture says, "In Him dwells all the fullness of the Godhead bodily" (Colossians 2:9). And, "He is the visible image of the invisible God" (Colossians 1:15). "We beheld His glory, the glory of the only begotten of the Father, full of grace and truth" (John 1:14).

Pastor John Bisagno said repeatedly throughout his long ministry, "Jesus Christ is everything God has to say about Himself."

The Lord Jesus Himself said, "He who has seen me has seen the Father" (John 14:9), and "When the Holy Spirit comes…He will testify of Me" (John 15:26).

The early believers were persecuted, not for preaching about God, but for speaking of Jesus. (Acts 4:18) Had they been silent about Jesus, there would have been no persecution.

A healthy church will always make much of Jesus.

9. Nothing is said about salvation, no one gets saved, the baptistery is dry.

Growing up on our Alabama farm, we had a pear orchard in the back yard. Over on the next ridge, my grandfather had a large apple orchard. Scattered throughout were peach trees. They all had one big thing in common: healthy trees gave us delicious and abundant fruit. Healthy fruit.

If the tree was barren or the fruit diseased, it was a dead giveaway that the tree was in trouble.

This is not to say that all churches taking in large numbers of new members and baptizing many hundreds are automatically healthy. To our shame, some use gimmicks to get people to join a church and manipulate them into being baptized. They resort to this rather than taking the harder, better road of building a healthy church.

I chose and appointed you that you should go and bear fruit, and that your fruit should remain.... (John 15:16).

10. Neither the members nor the leaders are willing to pay the price to make the church healthy.

Going from deathbed to vigorous health requires sacrifice, commitment, work, and often a certain amount of pain.

And, it takes time.

Making a believer healthy and a church strong will require a willingness to die to self, to give up doing things "our way."

Some choose to die rather than change.

Our Lord asked the man at the pool of Bethesda, "Do you want to be well?" (John 5:6).

Not everyone does.

Members and leaders alike should remind themselves daily of three great truths about the church:

—This is the Lord's Church. He died for it, I didn't. (Matthew 16:18)

It's not our church. Even if your grandpa helped to start it, it was never his and you didn't inherit it. Even when every member is related to one another, it's still the Lord's church and not a family heirloom.

—The single question therefore is "What does Jesus want done with His church?" (Acts 9:6)

Anyone who asks this of the Lord should be prepared to wait for an answer. "Wait upon the Lord" is a command found throughout Scripture. And waiting is hard work!

—Whatever we do for the church, good or bad, Jesus takes personally. (Acts 9:3,5; Matthew 25:40,45).

This may be one of the most surprising insights from Scripture. Hebrews 6:10 says, "God is not unjust so as to forget your work and the love that you have shown toward His Name, in having ministered to the saints and in still ministering." By ministering to the people of the Lord, we minister to Christ. He takes it personally.

We honor Christ when we bless His church.

CHAPTER FOUR

The Romans 12 Blueprint for Christ's Church

Think of this chapter as a template, a form (or pattern or framework) which may be laid over the entire 21 verses to describe God's plan for a healthy church.

The word "church" is not used in Romans 12. In fact, it's found only 5 times in the entire epistle, all in the final chapter. Yet, clearly the Apostle Paul is writing to all the Lord's churches in general and the one at Rome in particular.

Nowhere does the text call this a pattern for a healthy church. I would simply say that some things are so obvious it's not necessary to spell them out. It's a no-brainer. *The healthy church description in Romans 12 is one such.*

Scripture's blueprint for a healthy church has three sections...

FOUNDATION: Everyone is committed to the Lord. (Romans 12:1-2)

I beseech you therefore, brethren, by the mercies of God, that you present your bodies a living sacrifice, holy, acceptable to God, which is your reasonable service. And do not be conformed to this world, but be transformed by the renewing of your mind, that you may prove what is that good and acceptable and perfect will of God. (NKJV)

This is our vertical relationship. It comes before anything else. Without this commitment to our Lord, there is no church, period.

a) The mercy of God is the starting point. Everything we do is in response to all He has done. (See the previous verses, Romans 11:30-36).

The initiative is with Him; we are all responders. "We love Him because He first loved us" (I John 4:19). Only those who have come face to face with their own depravity and unworthiness can appreciate God's grace and mercy.

b) We commit our lives to the Lord God through Jesus Christ. We place ourselves on His altar every day of our lives. After our initial salvation experience, we daily recommit ourselves to Him. "I die daily," said Paul in First Corinthians 15:31.

No one should be living on remembered blessings or ancient grace. His mercies are new every morning (Lamentations 3:22-23).

c) We become focused on the will of God. Knowing His will and obeying it become our chief concern. "What will please the Father?" was the driving force of Jesus' earthly years. (Matthew 11:26 and Luke 10:21)

Summing up: All the Lord's people, but particularly leaders of His church, have been the recipients of His mercy, have committed their lives to Him, and are daily focused on becoming more like Him and doing His will.

FRAMEWORK: Everyone is growing in Christ. (Romans 12:3-8)

For I say, through the grace given to me, to everyone who is among you, not to think of himself more highly than he ought to think, but to think soberly, as God has dealt to each one a measure of faith. (vs. 3)

This is our internal relationship. In a house, the framework includes the massive timbers that form the rafters and joists, the underpinning and studs. In the completed house, these structures will remain invisible to everyone, but if they are absent or placed poorly, everything is in jeopardy.

Church members are healthy in relation to:

a) Themselves. They are humble, but not groveling (vs. 3). They have a solid, balanced view of themselves as sinners saved by grace, as objects of divine grace.

b) The body as a whole. They belong to the entire group and are not loners (vs. 4-5). They have a deep appreciation for the whole congregation, as well as for the people of God everywhere. The more they love the Lord, the more they treasure one another. When they backslide, their affection for each other will be the first casualty.

c) Their spiritual gifts. They accept their gifts and use them within the congregation in Christ-honoring and body-building ways (vs. 6-8). (See Paul's in-depth teachings on spiritual gifts in First Corinthians 12-14.)

Summing up: There is no place for solo acts and lone rangers within a healthy church. People see themselves as part of the Body of Christ. They do not exalt themselves above others. None are soloists but all are performers, so to speak, in the Lord's choir or symphony.

FINISHING: Everyone lives by the law of love. (Romans 12:9-21)

Let love be without hypocrisy. Abhor what is evil. Cling to what is good....

This is the horizontal relationship. With a house, the finish-work is what people see. They do not notice the foundation or the framework unless something is wrong. What they see will be the floors, walls, ceiling, and furnishings.

In a congregation, they will see the behavior of God's people toward one another, their outreach to the world and their work of ministry and worship.

Scripture does not stop with simply commanding love but explains what such love will look like. After all, scripturally, love is never an emotion, something we feel, but an action, something to be done.

Love is something we do.

If our love is pure and without guile or hypocrisy, among other things it will look like this:

a) This kind of love hates some things.

Followers of Christ will hate what He hated: bad religion, corrupt leadership, and hypocrisy. They do not hate the people; they hate what they have become.

An unhealthy church will love the things it should be despising and opposing. (Each person will have his own list for this. Mine would include alcohol, greed, abortion, living-together-without marriage, and sexual freedom.)

b) This kind of love values good things.

Scripture does not say "cling to what is religiously good." After all, "every good and perfect gift comes from Him" (James 1:17). God's people should appreciate any music, art, or other creative expressions that are truly good, and not restrict their approval to the religious, something Scripture never does.

An unhealthy church values unhealthy things.

c) This love puts others before itself (vs. 10).

Seek out and treasure the pastor and church worker who does this, and you know you have found a winner. To our everlasting shame, many in the ministry seem to make every decision by whether it will enhance our resume' and further our career.

An unhealthy church is beset by members vying for power and prominence.

d) This love is grounded in faithfulness to Christ (vs. 11-12).

This is its source, its reservoir.

An unhealthy church will skip the daily devotions and discipleship practices to get on with the program. Prayer is not exciting, so it goes by the wayside.

e) This love does kind deeds to all people, but particularly to fellow disciples (vs. 13).

Hospitality is a big deal in Scripture. See Hebrews 13:1-2 and Matthew 25:40,45. In the little Epistle of Third John, we see the brute Diotrephes forbidding church members from extending hospitality to traveling workers.

An unhealthy church does kindnesses only to the deserving and to the favored.

f) This love treats enemies kindly (vs. 14,17-20). This may be the most radical of our Lord's teachings and can also be found in places like Matthew 5:43-48 and Luke 6:27-38. We note that Jesus was not commanding warm fuzzy feelings, but selfless action. In commanding us to love enemies, He spells out what that means: We are to do good, bless, pray, and give to those doing us wrong.

An unhealthy church will vilify, ridicule, and attack its enemies.

g) This love blesses the hurting and the lowly (vs. 15,16).

No student of Scripture–and that should be all of us–can miss that the hurting and the lowly are favored by the Lord. And yet, they are the first to be deserted by an unhealthy church.

h) This love is an overcoming-with-good force (vs. 21).

An unhealthy church is often overcome by evil.

The Lord fully intends His people to show His kind of love toward those who do us wrong. Our natural instincts kick in here and we want to retaliate, to get revenge. The Lord's plan, however, is not to destroy an enemy but to show Him Christ, and even to win him. Even if the evildoer does not change, at the very least he will know he has come face to face with a genuine child of God. He will have no excuse when he faces God at judgment.

When we do loving things toward our enemies, we accomplish twelve good things:

--We honor God, please Jesus, and become instruments for the Holy Spirit for whatever He has going on here.

--We infuriate the devil, puzzle our enemies, and silence the church's critics. The enemy was expecting us to retaliate in kind. The last thing he was expecting was to be targeted by loving kindness.

--We bless the church, encourage other believers going through equally difficult times, and bear a strong witness to the watching world. Outsiders are drawn to Jesus when they see us behaving the way He did.

--Doing loving things to our enemies will bless us, will cause our anger to dissipate, and according to Luke 6:35, result in a great reward in Heaven.

Let us teach Romans 12 to our people as the model for a healthy church, and constantly keep it before them.

---ooo000ooo---

We delight in the way a single Scripture will have so many applications. Because this is God's word, it fits an endless variety of fascinating situations and needs. So, in no way do we mean to imply that Romans 12 is limited to our application above (as a blueprint for a healthy church).

For instance, the chapter calls for a wonderful balance for God's children...

Verse 9 -- a balance between love and hate

Verse 12 -- a balance between work and joy.

Verses 12-13 -- a balance between prayer and labor.

Verse 13 -- a balance between duties to members of the congregation and to outsiders.

Verse 15 -- a balance between rejoicing and weeping.

Verse 16 -- a balance between duties to the high and the low

Verses 18-19 -- a balance between peace and war.

The inimitable Warren Wiersbe used to say we need one more beatitude: "Blessed are the balanced."

Amen.

CHAPTER FIVE

Scripture Provides A Snapshot of a Healthy Church (Acts 6:1-7)

Many a pastor has given thanks for the problematic Corinthian church and Paul's epistle where he addresses its woes.

Learning that a first century New Testament church was beset by division, rivalries, controversies, immorality, and lawsuits keeps us from despairing that modern churches have all gone to the dogs.

From the beginning, the Lord's churches have struggled with these issues.

We are not saying misery loves company, or that we receive comfort from knowing we're not the first, only that we shouldn't panic and over-react.

We know the Lord is not surprised, nor does He give up on us when our churches do battle with the forces of darkness. It's a constant thing.

Question: Is there a church in the New Testament that got it right? That serves as a role model for all churches that would come later.

Yes, indeed. The church in Jerusalem as described in Acts 6:1-7.

This was a few months after Pentecost and things were booming. The church was growing, the apostles had all they could handle with discipling the new believers, and the community was enchanted by what they were seeing.

Suddenly, it all ground to a halt.

Here is our brief analysis.

Problem: The widows of the newcomer group--the Greek-speaking Jews--are being neglected in the daily distribution of food, in favor of the Hebrew-speaking widows.

How did his happen? In Acts 2 we learn that from all over the Roman Empire many thousands of Jews came for Pentecost. An untold number heard Peter preach the gospel. Three thousand responded and were saved that day.

Many of these must have decided that rather than rush back home, they should stick around to learn more about Jesus from the apostles.

That's how the church that started the day with 120 members (Acts 1:15) quickly became a mega-congregation (Acts 2:41).

No one had any experience in discipling vast numbers of converts, particularly this many so quickly. The disciples were writing the book on this as they went.

Acts 2:42 informs us that the daily activities of this congregation--this would be their discipleship program--

consisted of "the apostles' doctrine, fellowship, breaking of bread, and prayer."

While they didn't have the New Testament, they had the next best thing, the apostles. Teaching the new believers about Jesus--all they saw and heard during their three years following the Lord-- was great preparation for the time when certain ones would begin to put on paper (okay, parchment) the story of Jesus, which we call The Gospels.

At some point, the apostles got wind of a problem. The newcomer widows were being neglected in the distribution of food, in favor of the Hebrew (local) widows. Now, this should have been expected, but things were happening so fast no one had thought of this.

The temptation is to blame any conflict or division on the devil. But let's not do that. The enemy has nothing to do with this church's problem. This is all the result of church growth and nothing more.

It's a good kind of problem.

What is impressive is how quickly, how smoothly, and how effectively the church dealt with the conflict. After all, few things tell the story on church health like how it responds to a problem.

Look at these positive things about that church's health...

1. The apostles took the lead. They responded immediately. They did not sweep it under the rug, did not say "these things will take care of themselves," nor did they delay.

2. They involved the entire congregation. Rather than micromanage or dictate, the apostles asked the people to choose a team to deal with the problem.

3. The apostles would not stop their more important work ("prayer and the ministry of the Word") to "serve tables." While both were important, they knew their assignment and held to it. The Holy Spirit would have prepared and gifted others for such responsibilities.

4. The congregation responded well. Instead of placing blame or bickering about it, they obeyed their God-called leadership and chose seven men of high caliber.

5. Few things tell the tale on a church like the leaders it chooses. These were godly and mature people.

6. It appears that the seven chosen were from the minority, newcomer group since all the names are Roman and not Hebrew. The congregation was handing the matter over to representatives of the newcomers to deal with as they wished. The trust level was impressively high.

7. The apostles were still in the lead, however. Once the congregation chose the seven, they were brought before the apostles. While Scripture doesn't mention it, we may assume the apostles did a little "vetting," to make sure of the integrity

and maturity of each one. Then they laid hands on them and prayed.

8. Whatever the seven did--and we're not told exactly how they carried out their assignment--they did it so well and the effect was so well-received that the community and outsiders were drawn in. The watching world was making a statement of affirmation to this body of Christ: "We like the way you do things. We want what you have."

9. Even "a company of the priests were obedient to the faith," the ultimate compliment (6:7). If anyone was going to find fault and criticize, we assume it would have been the priests. But they were drawn to Christ by the activities of that healthy church.

As with this passage from Acts 6, the First Timothy 3 text giving the qualifications for deacons does not specify what they are to do. Personally, I find that liberating. It allows the pastors and deacons to work together in deciding what the church needs and what to do about it.

It's what healthy churches do.

For that reason, I suggest to deacons that they not set in stone (in their by-laws) their exact responsibilities, other than in a general way. Let their leadership meet with the pastoral team each year to prayerfully decide how the deacons can do the most good this year.

CHAPTER SIX

Nothing Tells the Story About A Church's Health Like Its Leadership

For two hours I had moderated a church business meeting where the pastor was fighting for his ministry. Various members spoke about his doctrine, sermons, pastoral work, leadership. Much of the criticism, I felt, was flimsy and unfair, but being the moderator, I stayed out of it.

They voted to terminate the pastor that night. Later as I exited the building, an elderly lady said, "This is the fourth pastor in a row we've done this to."

Few things signal that a church is diseased like a pattern of firing its leadership. Stated another way, the choice of leaders--lay and ministerial--will speak volumes about the condition of the church.

It won't tell the whole story, but a lot of it.

Not long ago I was speaking in the First Baptist Church of Long Beach, Mississippi. Pastor LaRue Stephens informed me that he had been there 22 years. Their 20-year minister of music was retiring that day. The church's minister of education has been there 12 years. The student minister, my long-time friend John Jones, was the newbie, at 10 years. Nothing speaks so eloquently about the health and stability of that church as the long tenure of its leaders. I would not be surprised to find that its lay leadership is solid and faithful in the same way.

How to assess a person's strengths

In Luke 16, our Lord gives three tests to judge the worthiness of a person. And since we are told not to "lay hands on someone hastily" (I Timothy 5:22), meaning leaders should prove themselves first, this is important.

He who is unfaithful in what is least is faithful also in much; and he who is unjust in what is least is unjust also in much. Therefore if you have not been faithful in the unrighteous mammon, who will commit to your trust the true riches? And if you have not been faithful in what is another man's, who will give you what is your own? (Luke 16:10-12).

Jesus suggests three tests: 1) Faithfulness in the little things. 2) Faithfulness with money. 3) Faithfulness in something borrowed.

LITTLE THINGS. When a boss tries to decide whom to promote, he/she looks around to see who is doing a good job where they are, who is ready to handle the bigger stuff?

In one church, I had trouble finding a competent administrative assistant. After a couple of aborted attempts at finding someone, we had a quick staff conference and decided to promote the church receptionist. In the twelve months she'd been on staff, she had proven herself. Shirley Bullard became an outstanding assistant and remained in the pastor's office over 20 years.

The pastor of a church down the road called me one day. "Joe, I feel my abilities are not being fully used in this little church. I'd like to pastor a bigger church. Can you help me?" I said,

"Jim, I'll be happy to pass your resume' on to a church but let me tell you what's going to happen."

"The first thing that pastor search committee will do is look to see what you are doing where you are serving. The only way they have to judge how you would do as their pastor is to see what you have done here. So, the best way to move to a big church--if that's what God wants--is to do a great job where you are."

It's not a new principle, although it may have been to him.

There is simply no way to shortcut this process.

FINANCIAL THINGS. How a person uses his money will tell a thousand things about his values, his self-discipline, and his heart. Our Lord Jesus said, "Where your treasure is, there will your heart be also" (Matthew 6:21).

I don't want someone in leadership at our church whose heart is not in it.

This is why pastors need to know--to some degree at least--what people are giving to the church. (I'm well aware there are so many ways a pastor could misuse that information. Please read on.)

Most churches have financial people who keep up with records of contributions and issue receipts for tax purposes. Confidentiality is a huge deal.

And a faithful pastor wants to minister impartially to every member, whether they give a dime or a million. That's one side of the coin.

On the other hand, the pastor and his leadership team need to know whether prospective leaders are trustworthy. Their finances are one huge part of the answer. (Not the only part, to be sure. And it's not just their contributions to the church, but overall financial faithfulness.)

Going back to Matthew 6:21--your heart follows your treasure--if a person has the money but is giving little or nothing to the Lord's work, it would be fair to say his heart is not in it. No right-thinking person would want him to lead the church or any portion of its ministry.

I'm well aware of the complaints this will generate. "Making decisions based on money? That's the problem with the church today!" "Sounds just like the world."

We are either going to be biblical or we're not. Your argument is with the Lord Jesus, I answer.

Each pastor has to decide.

One remedy...

My suggestion is a simple one. The administrator of the financial office should inform the pastor in general terms about a leader or prospective leader's giving record.

I used to hand our financial secretary a list of potential deacons. A few hours later, she returned the list with an indication by each name on whether the person could be considered as tithing their income to the church.

The risk of putting leaders in place whose heart is not in the Lord's work is too great to ignore. We've all heard of pastors discovering that the troublemaker in their church was giving next to nothing. A better scenario would have been to learn of his disobedience before promoting him to a place of influence.

In the same way, a pastor should know when their people do unusually good things in the Lord's work. If a wealthy person gives a million or some poor person works hard and makes a sacrificial gift of five hundred, the pastor should be told so he can acknowledge it in an appropriate way.

Our Lord and the disciples watched people bringing their gifts into the temple treasury.

Now Jesus sat opposite the treasury and saw how the people put money into the treasury. And many who were rich put in much (Mark 12:41-44).

That's how they spotted the faithful widow who was giving sacrificially. That one woman's faithful gift has inspired countless millions to do extraordinary things.

The Apostle Paul delighted in the Macedonian church's generosity and happily called attention to it.

...in a great deal of affliction the abundance of their joy and their deep poverty abounded in the riches of their liberality. For I bear witness that according to their ability, yes, and beyond their ability, they were freely giving, imploring us with much urgency that we would receive the gift and the fellowship of the ministering to the saints (Second Corinthians 8:2-4).

BORROWED THINGS. The church member who has abused the church van will not be given a larger assignment. The deacon who has not carried out his ministry to the widows and the needy will not be elected to lead the entire body. The pastor who is ignoring his flock and preaching stale sermons will not be asked to come to a greater and more demanding congregation.

Years ago, when I served as a trustee of our denomination's mission board, our travel expenses were reimbursed by the agency's treasurer. On one occasion it came out that a board member was double dipping. After being reimbursed by the mission board, he turned in receipts to his church to be paid by the treasurer. Once the congregation found this out, they fired him. As they should have.

It's not just the money. His unfaithfulness indicated a lack of character that disqualified him for the ministry, period.

Choose leaders carefully

Every church will have its own system of selecting lay leadership as well as ministers. The church which chooses deacons and committee chairs based on popularity is asking for all the trouble it's going to get. Scripture gives numerous qualifications for those chosen to lead God's flock. (Paul's writings in First Timothy is a primary source for this, particularly chapters 3 and 6.)

Nothing tells the tale on a church like the caliber of people it chooses as leaders.

PART TWO

Imagine we are walking inside and around the outside of the church, chatting about various aspects of the Lord's work. Sometimes it's positive and affirming, and sometimes we deal with the unhealthy stuff.

That's Part Two.

See if any of this touches your situation. Each chapter is self-sustaining, and they are not interconnected.

CHAPTER ONE

What to Do with The Problem of Immature Church Members

Grow in the grace and knowledge of our Lord and Savior Jesus Christ (2 Peter 3:18).

By this time you ought to be teachers, (but) you need someone to teach you the first principles of God and have come to need milk and not solid food (Hebrews 5:12).

A church leader was venting. "We have so many immature members. And the problem is, they want to stay that way!"

The leader said, "How do we deal with our discouragement? How can we keep from becoming Pharisees who constantly see their faults and not their potential? And how do we love those who cause so much trouble in the church by their immature actions?"

The letter concluded, "I feel like I'm in danger of becoming like the Ephesus church, the one which had lost its first love." A reference to Revelation 2:1-7.

My first thought upon reading the question was: "You're not alone, my friend. Every spiritual leader fights that same battle, although not to the same extent."

Let's do a quick study on the subject, then allow me to make some observations....

Paul saw the Corinthian church split asunder as a result of immaturity. He said, "I could not speak to you as to spiritual people, but as to carnal, as to infants in Christ." (First Corinthians 3:1).

Well. That was pretty plain. Wonder how they took that. (Paul was safely at Ephesus, and thus insulated from the barbs of the worst of the bunch.)

Paul continued, "I fed you with milk and not solid food.... For where there are envy, strife, and divisions among you, are you not carnal and behaving like mere men?" (3:2-3)

Their immaturity showed up in a number of problems which are dealt with throughout this epistle: lawsuits among members, immorality, splintering into cliques, favoritism, pride over spiritual gifts, etc.

What was Paul's remedy for these spiritual dwarfs? He reminded them of who they were in Christ. "We are God's fellow workers; you are God's field; you are God's building" (3:9). "Do you not know that you are the temple of God and that the Spirit of God dwells in you?" (3:16). "Let a man so consider us as servants of Christ and stewards of the mysteries of God" (4:1). Then, he said…

"I do not write these things to shame you, but as my beloved children I warn you" (4:14).

So, the immature in Christ need to be reminded of who they are in Christ, of what they might become, and the dangers of failing to be what God intends.

And they were to love. I Corinthians 13 stands as the gold standard of Christian behavior. Love covers a multitude of things, to be sure.

Okay. Here then are some observations on the problem of spiritual immaturity in a congregation…

(1) As long as a church is reaching new people for Christ, it will have immature members. So that part is good.

(2) The bad thing is when—as my friend wrote—the church is filled with the immature. When no one is growing, when the immature are calling the shots around there, the news is all bad.

(3) Ideally, a church will never select leaders from among the spiritual infants. But pity the pastor when the entire jury pool, so to speak, is filled with the immature. (One good thing about a larger church is that when some leader begins acting childish, others will speak up and not let them get by with it.)

(4) What to do about a non-growing church membership? Two suggestions:

–a. Find the few who seem to be open to growing in Christ—to trying something new, to studying the word, to making changes however tiny—and go with them. Put your emphasis on those who are responding but without neglecting the others. (In a garden, you fertilize the plants showing promise.)

–b. Find the least demanding spiritual disciplines you can and start there. Lead the infants to take baby steps first. What might that include? Here are some things that come to mind; you'll think of others...

Give everyone three printed invitations to some upcoming church program to hand out to neighbors, co-workers, extended family. (Anyone can do three! Surely.) Ask everyone to "Pause tomorrow at noon and pray for (whatever; the pastor or some upcoming event or someone in need)." (Just one time; it won't cost anything; everyone can do it.)

Tell the church of someone in the news who needs encouragement. Give them paper and ask them to write a note of love and hope and place in "this basket" and we will mail them all tomorrow. (Find small things. Easily done. But possibly with big impacts.)

(5) As for business meetings where the immature have been known to show their colors, leaders should go into these with lessened expectations. Quit expecting that "tonight everything will be perfect." Instead, even though you are praying for unity and harmony, be prepared in your mind for the carnal to make an appearance and not to let it bother you.

Pastors should be prepared for anything and plan to respond kindly and firmly. Stay the course, but do not stoop to the level of someone who is being unkind.

(6) Pray, pray, pray. Then pray some more. Make a list of a dozen or twenty members who need to grow or show some signs of responding and pray for them daily. Tell no one about your list. It's between yourself and your Lord. We can be

assured the Lord and you want the same thing here, so you are praying on solid ground.

(7) When you see positive developments, encourage the person. Do not say anything condescending ("Well, it's about time!" or "You're finally beginning to see the light!") but be sweet. "Thank you for what you said in the business meeting, Charlie. That was just right."

Drop him or her a quick note. Two sentences are sufficient, just enough to call attention to the value of what they did/said and to thank them.

(8) When you call on shut-ins or newcomers or visitors to your church, take along a member. Tell them they do not have to do anything, but you would like them to accompany you. The best way to catch fire is to stand close to something burning. Presumably, you are that something ablaze for the Lord. (My wife reminds me to say a pastor should take a man; a woman should take a woman.)

And one more: When you find yourself in a casual setting with a leader of another church ask, "What have you found that works in helping the immature to grow in the Lord?" I can almost guarantee you some of your ministry friends will have great ideas on this.

As always, keep your eyes on the Lord and not on the people. It is the Lord Christ whom you serve, said Paul in Colossians 3:24.

It's our faithfulness He seeks; the results are His business.

CHAPTER TWO

Let's face it. Some church people hang on to their jobs too long. In most cases, it's unhealthy.

"Diotrephes who loves the preeminence…" (3 John 9)

In one church I served, the assistant pastor had been there for over 25 years and was long past retirement age. After I learned he was working against my leadership and the lay leadership started talking about his retiring, I was happy to support plans to give him a good send-off.

We set a date, with his complete involvement, and the congregation provided a generous love offering. Then, just before the big day, the personnel committee informed me that they were asking him to remain in place. He would not be retiring.

Yes, they "informed" me; they didn't ask. (If you think this indicates problems on several levels, you'd be right.)

The assistant gladly stayed on, seeing himself as the savior of the church against this young whippersnapper of a pastor. (I was 46, not exactly a kid, but 20 years his junior.)

And no, he did not return the love gift. (Smiley face goes here.)

Why would he want to hold onto the job? It seemed to give him a sense of prestige being a prominent minister in the city's most storied church. That and a dollar or two would have bought him a cup of coffee.

If you conclude I had more problems in that church than just the assistant pastor, you would be correct. I ended up leaving after three years on less than ideal terms.

What's funny about that—sad funny—is that two years later, I heard the new pastor was trying to get him to retire and having a time of it. I had to smile.

The man was determined to hang on. He was in his mid-70s by then. (He's in Heaven now and must be glad to know it's a permanent position.)

There was a man in that church who chaired the building committee and frankly, did a good job of it. I had no problems with his leadership. However, he been appointed 35 years earlier by a pastor who retired the next year, and then kept it through the next three pastors. But now, after nearly four decades, the new pastor wanted him to step down, and he was resisting.

Why would he hold on to a position for four decades and not want to hand it over to someone else? Why would he not recognize the right of the pastor to appoint his successor?

Some years later, in my next pastorate, I recorded these things in my journal and added, "Whatever shortcomings my present church has, big shots throwing their weight around is not one of them." And then, "Thank you, Lord."

In one church I served, they still talked about two men who had dominated the church's business affairs for thirty years or more. One was Sunday School superintendent for over 30 years and the other church treasurer for a similar period. The way people talked about them; they were not chosen for their spirituality. Everyone was afraid of them. The leadership kept re-appointing them out of fear.

Imagine that: Leaders striking fear into the congregation. That has to be the silliest thing in the world. After all, what can they do to the people? To the Lord's church? And why would we let them?

All of this raises the question as to why some people hold on to church jobs long after their usefulness has come and gone? Long after the people want them in that position. Long after they should have stepped down.

A pastor friend told of a man who had dominated his small church for over 25 years. My friend, who was in his first pastorate at the time, did not know he was supposed to cow-tow to the guy. So, he called the man's bluff.

This fellow had run off the last two pastors. So now, he pulls the new little preacher off to the side and says, "Preacher, you stick with me, do what I tell you to do, and you'll have no problems in this church." The young pastor, green as grass but solid in his call from the Lord, said, "That's not how I understand the call of God, friend."

The day came when that deacon announced in a business meeting that he would be paying to have brick put on the outside of the new fellowship hall they'd voted to build. Everyone held their breath. This was not what they wanted. But no one dared cross the guy.

Well, one would. The green preacher.

The young pastor said, "Brother Gearshift, the church has already voted the building will be white asbestos shingles, just like the auditorium. So, we're going to have to reject your offering." And that tiny humiliation did the trick. The man left the church and never returned. The congregation felt like they had been let out of jail. There was a new spirit of joy and freedom in the church.

Why do people hold on to church jobs long after their usefulness has expired? long after the pastor wants them to? long after the congregation needs them in that slot?

—For some, it's power. Which is rather ridiculous, granted. What kind of power is it when one dominates 50 people? or even 500?

In the Robert Bolt play (and movie) *A Man for All Seasons,* on trial for his life, Thomas More confronts a weasel who had sucked up to anyone willing to offer him a position. Noting a medallion hanging around the man's neck, More asked what it represented. "It's for Wales," said the weakling. He had been appointed a high muckety-muck for Wales.

"Why Richard," More said, "it profits a man nothing to give his soul for the whole world…but for Wales?"

It was the perfect squelch. You gave up so much for so little.

–For some, it's the prestige. Another bit of silliness, to be sure. Does the world think the chairman of deacons/personnel/building/whatever of some church, large or small, is hot stuff? It does not, and that's just fine with the Lord of the Church. We are instructed not to love the world nor be caught up in its system.

–For some, it's the mistaken notion that no one else can do the job.

–Alas, for others that position has become their identity. If they are no longer the treasurer or chairman of this or that, who are they? My answer is: Let's find out. You might like the answer.

Such people have forgotten a lot of things. They need to be reminded that…

–They are not the whole body, but only one small member of it. An eye or a hand, or even a finger. See I Corinthians 12:14ff.

–They serve at the pleasure of the pastor and congregation. Again and again, Holy Scripture calls pastors the overseers of the flock.

–The church got along without them before they met them and will get along without them afterwards. (That's a corrupted version of a popular song from the 1950s.) Same with pastors, of course. And every other person in the church. Let none of us think we are indispensable.

–They--and the rest of us! --should read Luke 17:7-10 twice a day until it becomes part of our DNA. Thereafter, every day, we should look in the mirror and say to ourselves, "You are only an unworthy servant, just doing your duty." (This parable may be the most helpful tool our Lord gave for the unity of the church. It's found only here in Luke 17.)

–There are young people (meaning younger than them) coming along who need to learn to hold these jobs. In many cases, they will do them better and find new ways of blessing the church. And if that frightens anyone, too bad. Deal with it.

One final note....

From time to time, a pastor will tell me—as one did the other day—of a treasurer who has controlled the church purse strings for decades, and keeps the books at home, never allowing anyone to see them. My answer is always the same: That will go on as long as the congregation allows it. But the day some members begin to show some spunk (aka courage), they can end this.

As a rule, the best way to end it is by a new pastor who does not know any better just speaking up and calling for a new, improved procedure for handling finances. But he will have to hold his ground and have the support of a few key, determined members of his leadership.

In almost every situation like this, the secretive treasurer is hiding something. Usually, what is being hidden is not an illegality but incompetence. In any case, the leadership needs to end this little reign of terror.

In 2004, on becoming leader of the 130 SBC churches of the New Orleans area, I asked the administrative committee to hire an accounting firm to study how we were doing our finances and make recommendations. A few weeks later, they handed us a ten-page report recommending changes that would ensure the proper handling of God's money. It was a painless way to strengthen what we were doing, and no one was injured in the process.

(The background to that was that previously I had served as chair of the associational finance committee. At the time it seemed the finances were being handled correctly, but with one major flaw: The books were not open to inspection. There was no actual accountability. So, on taking office as the new DOM, I informed the finance committee that each quarter we would bring the checkbook into the meeting and let them see every check written. We would be transparent. Not long after that, when Hurricane Katrina flooded New Orleans and put many churches out of business, suddenly we began receiving hundreds of thousands of dollars in gifts to aid the churches. The Lord had led us to put sound financial practices in place before it became critical. Thereafter, there was not the first question as to how we were handling God's money.)

CHAPTER THREE

A Healthy Church Will Welcome Newcomers!

Welcome the stranger within your gates. For you were foreigners in Egypt. — Leviticus 19:10, 18, 33-34

This is one of the greatest frustrations and painful aspects of pastoring.

As the shepherd of the flock, you try to do well–prepare sermons blessed of God, lead your team to present effective ministries, build powerful worship services, develop disciples, and reach those in darkness. Then, your best people fail to do the smallest thing that could have made a world of difference.

They ignore the newcomer.

In fact, one of the biggest failures of our people is this: *They fail to think of the outsider.*

They're so caught up in their Sunday routine, they look right past the newcomers, the visitors, the first timers.

They're not bad people. These are the best people we know. But they are doing a bad thing.

In the decade of the 1990s, I pastored a church in metro New Orleans. Read my journal from Monday, March 22, 1999—

"I made a number of visits tonight. Left notes at three homes (no one there) and visited with Carol and Bob Coleman. They've been visiting our church several weeks. She said, 'We love it. Great music, etc etc—but only three people have greeted us!'"

"Three! Our people think they are friendly but in truth they are friendly to each other. Bob told me he had volunteered to help Clyde with cooking the wild game supper at church. Was brusquely turned aside with 'We already have enough help.' Then Bob came on to the dinner and brought a friend. One hour later, they were back. Said not a soul spoke to them. So disappointing."

That church had a reputation from the previous decade as strong on evangelism and soul winning. And they were doing many things right. As I say, these are good people, doing a bad thing.

More than once, our wonderful people opened their home (for several months at a time!) to mothers from Third World countries who were bringing critically ill infants to our Children's Hospital in New Orleans. They always responded well when I asked.

So, in turning away from the newcomers, they were not uncaring. They were just too busy. Too thoughtless.

Too unthinking.

They were preoccupied with their own plans, their own families, themselves. They were thinking about everything in the world other than the strangers and newcomers who were dying for some slight indication that they are welcome and wanted in this place.

I once stood before our people on a Sunday morning and held up two notes. "Both came in the mail this week," I assured them. The first was from a former member who had moved to another state. I read it to the congregation.

The woman said, "We've not found a church yet. The ones we've visited were not friendly at all. Not a single person spoke to us. We sure do miss you folks back at home. We loved the friendliness of our congregation."

I looked at our people and said, "Do we have a friendly church?" Heads nodded everywhere. They certainly thought they were friendly.

I said, "Now for the second letter. The writer is a newcomer to our city. 'Dear Pastor. We visited in your church last Sunday. Not a single person spoke to us. You have a most unfriendly church. We will not be back.'"

Both letters had arrived unsolicited in this week's mail.

I said, "We are indeed a friendly church. But only to one another. Not to outsiders or newcomers or first-timers."

"And there is a word for that. We are a clique. A little bunch of snobs."

We are snobs.

Sit in a Sunday School class where the members have all been best friends for thirty years. They know each other's phone numbers, birthdays, and the names of their grandchildren. Now, listen closely. The leader will say, "Didn't we have a good time at Elsie's house last week. This Thursday night, we're meeting at June's house. You all know what to bring. Don't be late."

As a visitor, you are lost. You don't know Elsie, have no idea where June lives, or what to bring.

They've just sent you a clear signal that this is a closed group, that they like their membership just the way it is, and you would not be welcome.

Churches often do a great job satisfying the members' needs for fellowship and togetherness. But we need reminding that we are not a fraternity or sorority, not a club and not a family reunion.

We are on mission for the Lord Jesus Christ, sent with the gospel message to reach the world for salvation and to disciple all who turn to Him in faith. The fellowship factor is a legitimate thing, but it must be inclusive and not exclusive. That is, we welcome the newcomer and first timer and do not exclude them or leave them no choice but to force themselves upon us.

We are on mission for Jesus Christ.

Our people will plan a great Christmas or Easter program. They will build sets and memorize lines and fill weeks with rehearsals. They will do everything right except two things: They often fail to get word to the community and limit their promotions to their own membership; and then, at the presentation of their program, they ignore all the newcomers and outsiders. They hug extended family members who came, ooh and ahh over one another's babies, and make plans to go out for pizza afterwards.

Meanwhile, the family filling the third pew on the right stands there isolated, looking around and waiting in the vain hope that some of these wonderful people will step across the aisle and show some indication that they are welcome in this place. They like everything about this church but one thing: They wish the people were friendly to strangers.

Read that and weep.

Now, in a perfect world, visitors and newcomers would not wait to be welcomed. They would know this is the House of God and they are welcome. They would rightly conclude that these good people are not uncaring, just unthinking.

We could wish those newcomers would keep coming to this church and would join it. And then–in this perfect world we're imagining–they could determine to make this a friendlier church and go out of their way to find newcomers and give them a hearty welcome.

The problem with that....

Even when people join the church and determine to make it friendlier, being new themselves they have no clue as to who is a member and who is the visitor. So they postpone their friendliness campaign until they know the membership. And by then, well, you know what happens....

By then, they have built their own little group in the church and have become satisfied and give little thought to people here for the first time today.

That's how it happens. It's how we fail the Lord.

The solution—and the only solution to my knowledge—is that the preacher must keep this before the people. Keep reminding them that they are not a closed group, but all are welcome, and that while they will no doubt find great friends in the congregation, they must work to become the same great friends to others the Lord will be sending this way.

Let the leadership find the sweetest people in the church-- that's the best way I can think of putting it--and enlist them as greeters. Give them assignments, training, and constant reinforcements.

It's a never-ending process. And a constant headache for the preacher, until he realizes it has ever been this way, and his work will not end this side of Heaven.

God help His church to get this right.

--ooOoo--

Dr. Bob Anderson pastored a great church in Baton Rouge. He told some of us of the time a Sunday School

class called to invite him to its Friday night cookout at a member's home. Bob had something going on at church that night but assured them he would come when he could. That Friday night, he finished his business at church and drove across the city. He found the street and was "pretty sure," he said, of the house hosting the cookout. He parked and walked up to the door. "One thing you know," he said, "in a cookout, no one is in the house. They're all in the back yard. So there's no need to ring the doorbell." He opened the door and walked in. Through the foyer, through the living room and dining room and into the kitchen. That's where he got two surprises. One, he did not know the woman standing at the sink staring at him. And two, he could see through the window above the sink there was no one in the back yard. He was in the wrong house.

Pastor Bob and the woman stood there staring at one another a long moment. "Nothing prepares you for how to handle this," he told us. Then, he blurted out, "I've come for fellowship!"

We all laughed, and he said, "You laugh, but that woman and her family ended up joining my church and became great members."

I've come for fellowship. That line could be printed out and hung around the neck of 95 percent of first-time visitors to our churches. No matter what they say they're looking for in a church, first of all they are wanting a congregation where the people love the Lord Jesus Christ, *love one another as Christ loved the church, and will welcome them into the fellowship. Nothing else is remotely as important as this.*

CHAPTER FOUR

In A Healthy Church, Leaders Will Be People of Courage!

"Be strong and of good courage" (said to or about Joshua seven times. Deuteronomy 6,7,23 and Joshua 1:6,7,9,18.)

Even in the difficult years of serving one particularly unhealthy church, it wasn't entirely bad.

My journal from those early, difficult years records a conversation with a deacon.

Deacon Ron said, "Pastor, you know that I voted against your coming to our church. But God has shown me that I was wrong. You have meant so much to me and my family."

We were talking about the church's lukewarm response to my first two years there.

It was a Sunday night and we had just completed a revival with a preacher who was as fine and godly as they come. His messages were anointed and straight from the throne. I had so wanted our people to hear God's message through him. But very few had turned out.

The problem--as they saw it--was his style. He was low key. He would stand at the pulpit with his hands in his pockets and speak in a conversational tone.

The congregation could not deal with that. Over the decades they had been conditioned to believe that powerful preaching is loud and bombastic, accompanied by guilt-inducing tirades and finger-pointing assaults. (They would have been so surprised to learn that Jesus sometimes preached sitting down in a boat!)

I said to the deacon, "Sometimes I wish God would send them a pastor whom they would respond to."

If that sounds like discouragement, it was.

Ron said, "I don't know why the crowd wasn't here tonight or why no one joined today. But, Pastor, this is far superior to the days when we used hook or crook to pack them in. I was conditioned that way for 15 years, and you don't break that overnight. But I'd rather have the group that was here tonight than a houseful who came to be entertained."

He said, "My wife can spot a pulpit committee a mile away. She comes home and tells me when we've had them. And Pastor, it would break my heart if you were to leave."

The journal records my reaction: "Wow."

This conversation came at a low time in the life of my lengthy ministry in that church. As it turned out, the Lord led Ron and his family to move across the state within a couple of years. But He left me there as pastor for another eleven years.

By the time God moved me on to the next assignment, it had become a far different church. Was it better, or stronger, or more faithful? I think so, but we will leave that to the Father, as we do everything else in this life!

But…

Looking back, I wish something.

I wish Deacon Ron had done something far more valuable to the church and to me personally than simply telling me how he felt.

I wish he had gone in front of the other 23 deacons and boldly told them what he said to me.

I wish he had had the courage to lay a speed bump in front of the little mob doing all it could to wreck what God was up to there. To speak against the lynching party that would meet in the church foyer before and after services to feed off each other's gripes and discuss how to get rid of the pastor whom God had sent.

I wish he had taken a public stand.

That he had been more courageous.

The church at that time had an odd mixture of deacons. They were a holdover from two previous administrations (you'll understand the term) and seem to have been re-elected annually by an undiscerning congregation that felt since this man is already ordained, he must be qualified. Some were; at least half of them were not qualified to crank the lawnmower.

Someone reading this will think I'm angry. I'm not. It's been many years and I've given a great deal of thought to that time, and this is as fair an assessment as I know how to give.

The majority of those deacons were anything but servants and did nothing in the church that I could see. Their sole function seems to have been to show up at the monthly meetings to pass along the gripes and complaints of the members who were their constituency. And since that group was wed to the ways of the past (see above reference to "hook or crook"), little I did met their approval.

Deacons meetings were unfailingly painful. Dissension was the order of the day.

Some kept insisting that Scripture puts deacons in charge of the church. After all, Acts 6 says the seven were chosen to "take care of this business." Those who felt otherwise kept silent.

When I said the deacons needed to be servants who looked after the needy in the congregation, you would have thought I was speaking in a foreign tongue. Even the best among them sat there in silence.

When the deacons vote to bring a recommendation before the church, I told them, common courtesy dictated that they should all be supportive. If one deacon could not support the recommendation of the whole body, he should not attack it before the church, since a deacon publicly opposing the deacons' own recommendation is disruptive to the church and fosters disunity. You would have thought I had urged them to take up a life of crime. "I fought in Korea for the right to speak my piece!" "I'm an American and no one is going to shut me up."

The good guys sat there in silence.

Most seemed not to get the concept of humility and submission and service. They thought being deacons meant they were in charge of the church and that the pastor should preach his sermons and leave the decision-making to them.

Looking back, I wonder...

What would have happened had my friend stood before them and told the deacon body what he said to me?

Wonder why he didn't?

–He didn't think of it? Just never occurred to him?

--He didn't think he had the right?

–He thought of it but didn't have the courage to endure the hostile reaction his words would have provoked?

I don't know.

What I do know is this:

–a) to stand before a runaway group of lay leaders and call them down takes real courage;

—b) for a layman to do this is far more effective than the pastor doing it, as he would be seen by some as being defensive and combative since dissension in the church almost always targets the preacher;

—c) even if that deacon's courageous confrontation before the whole group did not end the opposition, it would still have an effect. Some would listen.

Nothing encourages an embattled pastor like a leader standing up for him before his critics and speaking up.

We need more leaders who are unwilling to sit and do nothing, to fold their hands while the world goes to hell, to remain silent while the enemy holds the field. To stand before the misguided and ill-informed of their own group and call them down. Or wake them up.

In calling for courage, we need to say that sometimes godly and courageous church members will need to confront their pastor. I admit with a certain degree of shame that some churches are torn asunder by ungodly or carnal pastors who either were never called by God in the first place or who long ago jumped the rails and have gone rogue.

Let the leadership be strong and do the right thing.

We may or may not make a difference by speaking up.

One thing we do know: by remaining silent, our life counts for little, and the enemy wins the day.

---ooo000ooo---

I was reading the minutes of church business meetings from the First Baptist Church of Columbus, Mississippi, from the first decade of the 20th century. In one meeting, General Stephen D. Lee took the floor to resign. "These deacons don't want to do anything," he said. He told how when he was in the military—he was a West Point grad, a leader in the Army of the Confederacy, and the founding president of nearby Mississippi State University—he delighted when he could command his people to "Charge!" But he did not want to be part of a group content to sit and do nothing. The General was asked to hold off on his resignation until they could talk with him. The next month's minutes indicate that General Lee had reconsidered and would remain. The next year, the pastor resigned, a new preacher came in, and when the decision was made to tear down the 1838 structure and erect a new modern sanctuary, the man chosen to lead the effort was General Stephen D. Lee. A man of courage and action.

CHAPTER FIVE

What to Do When Church Members Insist on Their Rights.

"Why not rather be wronged?" (I Corinthians 6:7).

Pastors hear it all the time. Variations on this theme are endless...

--"I pay my tithe and I have a right for my minister to (do whatever he's insisting on)."

— "All these years we have belonged to this church and given our money to support these preachers, and now when we need him, he's in Israel on a Holy Land tour!"

— "I went by the church. I needed to see the preacher then, not the next day. And you're not going to believe this, but he was on his way out the door, headed to his son's little league game! And me a member of his flock. What kind of preachers are we getting these days?"

— "The preacher needs to apologize to me for what he implied in that sermon on Sunday. I know he was talking about me, even though he used someone else's name."

—And then there is this one, a true story from my journal....

The fellow said, "I called the church office and told them my dad was dying. Now, I'm not a member of the church but my parents used to be. They deserve better treatment than this."

(And what treatment did they receive?) "The pastor sent his wife, and she said something about him having to teach a Bible study then and he would be by later." (Did he come later?) "He came two hours later." (And did your father die?) "Well, not then. He died a few weeks later, but I was angry. When I call for the pastor to come, I expect him to come." (But you're not even a member. You don't even live here, and you had never met the pastor. Yet, you are angry?) "You bet I'm angry. I have a right to expect the pastor to earn his pay."

The stories every pastor could tell. But won't, for obvious reasons.

Pray for your ministers.

This is why the Lord has to call people into this work, instead of them lining up to volunteer. I tell preachers it's why they pay us the big bucks.

Church members who insist on their rights—the very idea is mind-boggling—would do well to remember what an elderly lady told a deacon who kept insisting in a business meeting that "I just want what's coming to me."

"Sit down, Henry. If you got what was coming to you, you'd be in hell."

Sad to say, pastors also insist on their rights…

—Look at what they're paying me. I've not had a raise in three years.

—I deserve better treatment than this. (Think of Moses in the wilderness. How many times did He bellyache to the Lord for calling him to lead this bunch of disorganized, self-centered, shallow ex-slaves to some place where they'd never been but had only heard of!)

--"It was my tenth anniversary and they did nothing. Not the first recognition! I'm humiliated."

— "Lord, I've done nothing but love them and serve them. And this is the thanks I get!"

Pastors call me with these complaints. They know I'm on their team as a veteran pastor myself.

In many cases, my counsel is the same: "Try to hang in there. Your reward is just ahead, and you will be so glad you were faithful." Do that, Jesus said, and "I will give thee a crown of life."

Consider Jesus.

Consider Him who endured such contradiction of sinners against Himself lest you also grow weary and lose heart. (Hebrews 12:3)

If our Lord had insisted on HIs rights—what He deserved and had every right to expect and ask and even demand—a lot of things would be different…

—He would have called ten thousand angels and put a stop to that Jerusalem foolishness. (See Matthew 26:53).

–He would never have gone to the cross for you and me. He would not have endured the taunting and spitting and blasphemy. (see Matthew 27:27-44) He would have made short work of them all.

–And He never would have loved people like you or me. He Himself knows our frame (Psalm 103:14) and knew we were made of humble stuff and were prone to fail.

He would have written earth off as a bad experiment and moved on to Planet X.

"But He died alone…for you and me." (That gospel song alluded to above.)

When you and I insist on our rights…

–We are showing ourselves carnal.

–We are shaming the Savior.

–We become part of the problem for the Lord's church instead of part of its answer.

–We hold the gospel up to ridicule before the world. "Look at that bunch. They're just like the rest of us."

–We show the Lord's teachings mean absolutely nothing to us. He said, "Do good to those who hate you. Bless those who curse you. Pray for those who mistreat you. And whoever hits you on the one cheek, offer him the other also." (See Luke 6:27ff)

And He went further with this thought. "Whoever takes away your coat, don't withhold your shirt either. Give to everyone who asks of you. And whoever takes away what is yours, do not demand it back."

On and on Jesus went, calling for loving actions that offend the carnal mind and demonstrate something far superior is going on with these who are His redeemed.

Jesus is always the final word on any subject…

He has the final word; He is the final word.

For you have been called to this purpose, since Christ also suffered for you, leaving you an example for you to follow in His steps. Who committed no sin, nor was any deceit found in His mouth? And while being reviled, He did not revile in return; while suffering, He uttered no threat, but kept entrusting Himself to Him who judges righteously.

For He Himself bore our sins in His body on the cross, that we might die to sin and live to righteousness; for by His wounds you were healed. For you were continually straying like sheep, but now you have returned to the Shepherd and Guardian of your souls. (I Peter 2:21-25)

Only those who believe God's word and are willing to leave their case with Him will be able to absorb a hurt and ignore a wrong done to them and go forward with a song on their lips.

Only the faithful.

CHAPTER SIX

20 Steps Toward Awakening A Sleeping Church and Stirring It to Action

"Awake thou that sleepest and arise from the dead, and Christ shall give thee light" (Ephesians 5:14).

A pastor I know has a problem. It's not unlike that experienced by many others, I imagine.

He has deacons who are undisciplined, church members who do not take care of the hurting, and in general, a congregation of unmotivated people. When he preaches evangelism or discipleship or community ministry, the way they sit there staring makes him wonder if the language he's using might be a foreign tongue to them.

Sound like your church? Sounds like several I've known.

Leaders need to know this going in: This is an uphill task, to awaken a sleeping church. If it were easy, every pastor would do it and no church would be stagnant or declining.

Here are my recommendations, not as an expert on anything, but as a veteran pastor with scars to prove I've been where you may find yourself at the moment.

Since every church is both similar and different, we will use a lot of generalities and broad-sweeping statements. You'll want to take anything that fits and skip the rest.

One. The bad news: You will encounter this same problem to one degree or another in every church you serve. No church is without the sleeping, the dormant, the complacent. It's the human thing. In high school physics we learned that a body at rest prefers to remain at rest, while one on the move wants to keep traveling. Inertia.

So, the question is how to arouse the church that seems cemented to the floor, then get it up and going.

Two. Plan to stay at it. This will be a marathon, not a sprint.

Leaders must not become discouraged by those who sit and stare when they should be receiving the message for what it is, a holy word from the Heavenly Father. We must not let the lack of response—or worse, a negative reaction—dishearten us. The harvest is worth the effort. "Be not weary in well doing," said the Apostle. "In due season we shall reap.... if we don't quit" (Galatians 6:9).

Assume this is not going to be accomplished by sunset. Plan for the long haul.

Three. Get your eyes on the Lord and keep them there. Whether the church is responding and growing, or ignoring you and fossilizing, leaders who want to make a lasting difference must stay focused on the Lord Jesus Christ. We do that in a hundred ways: staying in the Word personally, staying on our knees daily, self-talk (Psalm 116:7 is a favorite example), and continually bringing all we do and all who depend on us before the Father.

Four. Go with those who respond. The good news is some people will respond more quickly than others. Go with those who are listening, who show up, who want to move out and obey the Lord.

Put another way: Do not wait for the entire congregation to sign up before you do anything. Get this vehicle moving and others will climb aboard. And even if they don't, don't punish the faithful by making them pay for the sins of the dormant.

Five. Stay positive. Never fuss, complain, or harass your people. Likewise, encourage those who are responding not to criticize the ones who aren't. That's a strong temptation they will need to guard against. All the negativism will accomplish is to further harden the resistance of the pew-dwellers. They should encourage them to "come join us; we're having a great time."

Remind your team this is not the work of a few weeks, but a lifelong project and they should stay with it. The fruit is worth the effort.

Six. Start small. Think of starting a fire. You gather a small amount of the most flammable material you can put your hands on—pine kindling, a fire log, shavings, or a newspaper. You strike a match. The old campfire chorus says, "It only takes a spark to get a fire going; And soon all those around can warm up in its glowing...."

Remember the parable of the mustard seed. (Matthew 13:31-32) God loves to start small. When He began to save a world, He sent a Baby.

"Starting small" might mean leading a home Bible study. It could mean taking a few leaders to a nearby city for an important conference. Perhaps it's starting a senior adult choir. The choices are limitless.

Seven. Look around. Ask yourself: Who in the church is most on fire for the Lord? in love with His word, truly worshiping, sharing their faith? Who is already experiencing revival? Where is God already blessing this church? Do I see His hand at work in any particular place?

That's the starting place. Encourage those people. Pray for them.

Eight. Pray, pray, pray. Get more serious about prayer than you have ever been in your life. How much to pray, how long, or how intense--that's all up to you. Do it your way. But remember that "the effectual *fervent* prayer of a righteous person availeth much" (James 5:16). "Fervent" means you care deeply and are praying intensely.

Enlist a few prayer warriors from within the congregation as well as outside it. This could include people you've known in previous churches, who can touch Heaven with their prayers, but will not talk about this to others. Get them praying and keep them informed. (Note of caution: Never tell your prayer team anything you don't want repeated. A lesson learned the hard way!)

Nine. Preach Jesus. Don't talk or preach about revival. Talk and preach about Jesus, about loving Him and obeying Him and being found faithful. If He is lifted up, He will draw all men to Himself (John 12:32).

The temptation is to preach on revival, on some of the great revivals in Scripture, on awakening the sleeping church, and such. My own experience--and that's all this is--is that this is backwards. Preach Jesus. Do the best job you possibly can in declaring the whole counsel of God.

Ten. Wait on the Lord. As you pray, wait and watch for the Spirit to do things in answer to your prayers—perhaps to send a key leader who will be a great influence, to start a small movement with great potential, to make some change in you. Stay alert. "Wait on the Lord, be strong, let your heart take courage. Yes, wait upon the Lord" (Psalm 27:14).

David said, "I waited on the Lord and He heard my cry…" (Psalm 40:1). He may have been waiting, but he was crying at the same time. Our Lord told the disciples to "watch and pray" (Matthew 26:41). That's the same idea. We can wait and watch while remaining on the job. (see Nehemiah 4:17)

Eleven. Consider seeking outside help and counsel. If you're having no results, and you know a dynamic, successful leader whom God has used in significant ways, invite him/her to visit your church and make recommendations. Or you travel to their city and interview them. (In the interview, take notes, ask more questions, thank them, and leave.) What you do with their suggestions is between you and the Lord. Write a note of appreciation (and, enclose a check if they gave you significant time) immediately on returning home. One cautionary note: If the consultant offers to be available for further meetings, promise nothing. Your major adviser is the Holy Spirit, and you will be seeking His counsel on what to do next.

Likewise, unless God leads, I do not suggest you give that visiting "expert" a week or weekend with your congregation for some kind of focus or self-study. Do that and as pastor you are now pushed off to the side. Even though the Holy Spirit makes the pastor the overseer (Acts 20:28), you could be sidelined by the advice of the expert and the too-quick enthusiasm of some of your members. Announce to such people that "I don't believe we should do what the consultant recommended," and they may turn on you.

Best for pastors to do their job and remain in the driver's seat. (Unless God leads otherwise. These are general principles.)

Twelve. Write lots of notes. When someone does something well, write and tell them so. On Sundays, jot down names of those who will receive notes from you that week. Then, Sunday afternoon or Monday morning, get to it.

The notes, incidentally, need be no more than a few handwritten sentences, just enough to say, "Your solo in church was wonderfully used of the Lord, Kristi. I saw people with tears in their eyes. Thank you for blessing us." Or, "Bob, the breakfast you cooked for our men's meeting was outstanding. Thank you for getting up at 4 a.m. and setting such a great example of faithfulness and diligence. You are a blessing to your pastor."

People get so few letters these days that yours will stand out. They'll keep it for a long time and read it a dozen times before dropping it into a drawer.

Thirteen. Write nothing negative. When problems demand your attention, deal with them personally or over the phone. Write nothing negative in a letter. If you do, you will find that paper will long outlive whatever problem prompted it. Satan will delight in using this to slander you, stir up dissension, and arm your opposition with plenty of ammunition. I have scars from violating this!

Fourteen. Stay at home. No absentee pastor ever grew a great church. The minister who is out of the pulpit a great deal—preaching in other churches, leading groups to the Holy Land, attending conventions, taking extended vacations—is not giving his congregation the hands-on leadership they need. In time, after the congregation is thriving and a good leadership team is in place, you will be able to take those vacations and preach in other places, but only as God leads.

Fifteen. Set the standard. Become the role model for what you hope to accomplish. Visit in the homes of your church members and love on them; knock on the doors of people you hope to reach for Christ; make your daily devotional life the gold standard for your congregation. You cannot expect your people to grow beyond what their leadership is doing. If you want them to be generous, you start giving. If you expect them to witness, you share your faith.

Do not tell the congregation that you are now giving sacrificially or knocking on the doors of so many prospects each week. Keep it to yourself. The Lord will know. And when your people find out—as they will—God will use that to motivate them.

Sixteen. Ask, watch, listen. Be constantly searching for ideas. Read widely, and not just from the mega-church preachers. In your public library, check out the magazine section. Scan the contents of publications you never heard of, in search of fascinating subjects and interesting articles to prompt your own thinking. Attend conferences of other denominations that meet in your area. Sit there and listen. Take notes. Pick the brains of successful people in many fields.

I spent an unforgettable hour in a hospital waiting room while the wife of my deacon had surgery. I wanted to learn how C. C. Hope, Jr., went from being an unknown banker to president of the American Bankers Association, and later receiving an appointment by President Reagan as one of three commissioners of the FDIC. I've benefited from his insights a hundred times.

Seventeen. Expect setbacks. Ask any pastor of a thriving church and you'll hear this same tale: Somewhere along the road to health, the church went through a crisis or two in which some members grew upset and left.

In the typical scenario, the disgruntled members said cruel things about the pastor on their way out the door, predicting the church was going to perdition, and warning that without their money this church was never going to make it. The best revenge, as they say, is living well. The church had to get back up and get going again, but they did, and they're now able to tell the story.

Don't be surprised when this happens.

Church leader, you are not going to grow a great church without pains. Expect some to say they liked the church better when it was dead ("we had a family spirit then, but now I don't know who all these people are!"), some to accuse you of making changes (well, hello!), and some to fabricate stories or manufacture reasons to leave.

Let them leave.

John Maxwell says, "If you make no changes, the winners will leave. If you make changes, the whiners will leave. So, decide which group you want to keep."

Eighteen. Be selective. Be slow to choose staff members and lay leaders. Go for quality, not quantity. Best to have the part-time work of someone truly gifted and committed than the full-time efforts of a lazy, dull minister. (The stories I could tell!)

Remember the concept of *Holy Vacancies*: Leave a position open until the Lord fills it with someone He sends.

Nineteen. You will never arrive. Do not expect there to come a time when you can check "awaken a sleeping church" off your list of things to do. There will always be pockets of resistance, members who haven't opened their Bibles in years and are determined not to do so, and new babes in Christ who need to be grown and nurtured. Your work will never end.

Therefore, be cautious about announcing to the church that "We are now in revival" or "We have arrived!" Always press forward to the goal (Philippians 3:14), but keep in mind you will not reach it in this lifetime.

Twenty. Experiment. Do not get too comfortable with something that is working today. Ask Shoney's Restaurants or K-Mart or Sears--all companies that failed to adapt and stay fresh. You are always searching for ways to do things better.

Rick Warren says at Saddleback Church they never use the word "change," since some find that word threatening. "We say we're going to experiment," he says. "If this thing doesn't work out, we'll try something else. That way, no one is threatened."

Beware of gimmicks, church leader. Beware of quick solutions to deep-seated problems. Beware of doing a thing just because some hot-shot preacher or know-it-all layman told you it's the only way.

Never forget, it's His church. "I will build my church," Jesus said (Matthew 16:18).

Give Him the chance to do that where you serve.

CHAPTER SEVEN

What People Want from The Pastor and Have A Right to Expect

I hesitate to say any group in the church has a "right" to expect anything of another. Insisting on our rights almost invariably results in resistance, frustration, anger, and division. And yet believers who support the work of the Lord with their tithes and offerings and time and energy have a right to expect certain things from their shepherd. That's what this is about.

What follows is directed primarily to pastors. Others may listen in, but no one should miss the "they do not have a right" which comes at the end of each section.

If I got what I deserve, I'd be in hell. And so would you. So, let's not play the "I have my rights" card.

No one is entitled.

The Christian life is not about getting our rights or having others meet our demands. Far from it.

We have died with Christ. We are called bondservants and instructed to submit to one another. That is a far cry from the high and mighty calling the shots and running the church.

Nevertheless, when people go to the trouble to come to church with their families, often at great inconvenience, and remain with the program year after year through the good and the bad, it is not unrealistic for them to expect a few basic things to be present.

One. People want to hear a thought-provoking sermon on Sunday. They have a right to this.

Therefore, a faithful pastor will give priority to preparing the sermon and attention to delivering it effectively. The hour of worship is the best opportunity in the week to touch the largest number of members. Therefore, this should receive priority.

No one has a right, however, to expect the sermons to compete with the celebrity television preacher for entertainment value.

Two. People want to hear a message thoroughly biblical, consistent with the teachings of the Lord Jesus. They should hear that.

The pastor should know the Word and work at knowing it better. Study helps are available and great commentaries easily accessed. With every seminary offering online courses these days, the minister has almost no excuse for not being a Bible scholar.

However, the people do not have a right to expect every sermon to be at a high level of scholarship. The typical congregation is made up of children, youth, parents and seniors, the highly educated and the less educated, singles and married, rich and poor, and sometimes several racial groups. What touches one may miss another. Not every message will speak to each person in the same way, so we should be extremely careful in criticizing a sermon because "it did not meet my needs."

Three. Even if what they are hearing is the traditional message on a subject, they are well-familiar with, worshipers want it fresh and relevant to their lives. This is not unreasonable.

Pastors do well to stay attuned to things happening around them that could sharpen the focus and deepen the impact of the sermon. A child's off-the-wall comment or a slip-up from a celebrity or an item in today's paper may trigger something in the minister's mind to enhance the message.

However, no church member has a right to demand this. Some pastors come by this easily and naturally, while others have to work hard to connect the biblical word with the daily lives of the pew-dwellers.

Four. People want their pastor to be prayerful. They will be asking for intercession for their own needs and concerns, but they also need confidence that the preacher is living in the power of the Holy Spirit. This is good.

Pastors will want to pray without ceasing. They will want to set aside time every day for concentrated prayer, but also to send up "prayer arrows" as they travel, work, and play. The wise pastor will always be working to learn to pray more effectively.

However, no one has a right to check out a pastor's prayer life. This is a matter between the minister and the Lord.

Five. People want their pastor to be moral in every way Scripture teaches. If the preacher is single, they expect celibacy; if married, faithfulness. No minister may insist that what he/she does in their private time is their own business. They have no private time which is not the concern of their flock.

Pastors will want to work to be strong, disciplined, and yielded to the Lord. A wise pastor will have mentors to counsel him and will enlist a few prayer warriors to intercede for him regularly.

However, as a rule, church members do not have a right to inquire about the goings-on in the pastor's home, or about the relationship of the pastor to his spouse. (The exception would be when legitimate questions arise about the minister's ethical or moral behavior.)

Six. People want their pastor to be law-abiding and patriotic. We expect ministers to pay taxes and respect the government.

When a pastor is constantly running down the government and its leaders, some in the pew will feed upon that. Not everyone in the church has good mental health or is interested in obeying the Word. But humble men and women of God will soon grow uncomfortable with such antics.

Scripture commands us to obey the government, honor the king, and pray for those in authority. While it's true we must "obey God and not man," our focus should always be on serving the Lord and preaching His word. The government is neither our salvation nor our biggest problem.

A pastor will work to stay on course, seek professionals to help with taxes and investments, and obey the laws. Even if the membership does not inspect his tax records, they should be so well-done that he would not hesitate to show them if it became necessary.

However, the members do not have a right to see the pastor's tax records, any more than he has a right to see theirs.

Seven. The members want their pastor to be a leader of confidence and authority, but they also want him to be accountable to a few of the church leaders. Everyone benefits from this.

The pastor who exercises authority over the entire church but without accountability to anyone for anything is being set up for trouble. The most loving, responsible and faithful gift for a new pastor may be a small, representative group of members who will stand by his side in good times and bad. If he is doing wrong in some way, they will be the ones to hold him accountable and speak up.

However, the members do not have a right to boss the minister, to hold him to a time schedule, or to expect a report on how he spends his time, whom he visits, etc. The exception would be when he is clearly lazy and lax in his pastoral duties.

The list is probably endless. Church members want their pastors to be paid well, but it is not best for the members to decide such matters on the floor of a monthly business meeting. They should have a finance, personnel, or administrative committee to represent them in making these decisions.

Pray for your ministers. Love them. Support and encourage them. Remember the Lord Jesus said that whoever receives them is receiving Him (Matthew 10:40). When we honor the Lord's servant, He takes it personally.

Above all, let us be faithful in serving the Lord Himself. And that will be more encouraging to God's servants than anything you do during the time set aside for pastor appreciation.

--oooOOOooo---

I believe the Lord takes personally what people do to the servants He sends (see Matthew 22:1ff and Hebrews 6:10).

I have said to Joanne Keeling Burchfield that when her mother, the wonderful Ethel Keeling, arrived in Heaven many years ago, I believe the Lord Jesus Christ said to her, "Thank you for my coat."

I tear up at the memory.

It was my first church following seminary. Margaret and I were dirt poor and Greenville, Mississippi's Emmanuel Church did not offer much in salary. That first winter, I was doing a funeral. The rain was falling and the temperature dropping. Everyone was cold, wet, and miserable. I was wearing my only suit, a summer weight, that I'd had since we were married. It took a beating that day.

After the funeral, I drove home and changed into dry clothes and returned to the church office. Inside the door on the desk lay a large package from a men's clothing store. Inside was a gorgeous, black London Fog all-weather coat with a zip-out lining. It was the most beautiful thing I had ever seen.

Mrs. Keeling had watched her young pastor shivering in the cold and had driven straight to the department store and done something that would never cease to bless him.

That was fifty years ago, and it remains the kindest thing anyone has ever done for me.

CHAPTER EIGHT

What We Wish for The Lord's Church

That He might present it to Himself a glorious church, not having spot, or wrinkle, or any such thing, but that it should be holy and without blemish (Ephesians 5:27).

The Lord wants the best for His Bride. And so does every right-thinking child of His.

Here is my wish list for the church of the 21st century....

One. I wish the church were less of a business and more like a family.

Our Lord looked around at His disciples and followers and said, "Behold, my mother and my brothers! Whoever does God's will is my brothers and sisters and my mother" (Mark 3:33-35). The obedient are His family.

I'm so glad I'm a part of the family of God. The local church should be a smaller expression of that larger, forever family. I wish more of them were.

A real family nurtures its members, is always there, makes a big deal of each one's special moments, and puts each other ahead of anyone else or anything else. To paraphrase Robert Frost, "A family is where, when you have to go there, they have to take you in."

Families are not about numbers, divisions, classes, and groups. Family members are related by blood and joined at the heart. They weep when one of their number weeps, rejoice when they rejoice. They don't compete, except in a fun way, and are proud when one is honored.

People will often hesitate before joining a new church simply because they are in effect joining a family. Their unasked question is "Do I want to be family with these people?"

A business, on the other hand, functions by the bottom line. It turns out a product. It hires and fires people. But what business do you know that is run by faith and directed by prayer and motivated by love? The church is not a business but a family. When we who are the church fail to love and to care, we have reneged on our assignment, violated our mandate, and betrayed the Savior.

I wish my church were more like a family.

Two: I wish the church were less like the world and more like heaven.

Heaven values lasting things. You like gold? Why, up there they pave the streets with it.

Heaven loves diversity. Heaven's citizenship is composed of "every nation and kindred and people and tongues…" (Revelation 7:9).

Heaven is in the business of joy. As C. S. Lewis put it, "Joy is the business of heaven." The very atmosphere of heaven is joy

(Psalm 16:11). The kind of joy the world gives turns out to be artificial, superficial, and temporary (see Psalm 4:7).

Heaven is about serving God, about singing and praising and loving and rejoicing. The world is about using people to get our pleasure and griping when we don't.

Heaven doesn't sweat the little things and knows what really matters.

Alas, too many churches are more a mirror of the world's values than a statement of Heaven's verities.

Three: I wish the church were less like a club and more like a ministry.

Clubs are mostly about camaraderie and cliques and excluding those not acceptable. Christian love opens its arms to everyone.

Club members greet each other and welcome one another and take friends out to lunch. But ministry reaches out to everyone. God told Israel to welcome the stranger within your gates. "For you were strangers in Egypt" (Leviticus 19).

History tells of a time that St. Bernard returned to the monastery one evening with a long, drooping face. He had not found anyone to rescue that day, and he was sad.

"Jesus went about doing good" (Acts 10:38).

In the cemetery, Chuck Swindoll's mother saw a young woman weeping near a marble tombstone. She went over and told the woman about Jesus. Her heart was tender and open, and she came to Christ. As a result, that young widow began a graveyard ministry, looking for grieving hearts. Swindoll said she has led hundreds to Christ this way.

Four: I wish the church were less like a police force and more like a hospital.

A police force focuses on catching lawbreakers. Hospitals are into healing.

I'm not sure who gets credit for first saying it, but for me, it was Dear Abby who famously said, "Churches should not be museums for saints but hospitals for sinners."

"Lord," the Pharisees said, "your disciples are doing that which is not lawful." They are plucking grain on the Sabbath. Healing on the Sabbath. Walking too far on the Sabbath. They are laughing and you know that's not allowed around here. As for dancing, well, don't even ask.

"That one cigarette will send your soul to hell." A woman told me this statement came from her sister-in-law, a member of a harsh, legalistic denomination. She replied to the sister-in-law, "Then, explain something to me. You have told me that you hate your mother. That's a direct violation of God's commandment. And yet, my one cigarette will send my soul to hell. Explain that." She couldn't.

Disciples of the Lord Jesus Christ were sent to share His Good News with everyone, not to catch people doing wrong. Why do so many people miss this?

"The eyes of the Lord roam to and fro in the earth that He may strongly support those whose heart is completely His" (2 Chronicles 16:9). How good is that! And yet, it's directly the opposite of the enemy's slander that goes, "God's gonna get you for that!"

Let God's people reflect His love and share His message.

Pastors and teachers will need to keep stressing the proper (i.e., Scriptural) role of the church, its identity and purpose.

After all, churches tend to drift downward....

—away from family love-and-fellowship toward becoming a business.

—away from ministry reaching-out toward becoming a club.

—away from Heaven's values toward mimicking the world.

—away from caregiving toward law enforcement.

We must always work at staying alive and fresh and responsive to the Holy Spirit. "New Wine." Trying new things. Discarding outdated methods no longer working. Aggressive in reaching out. Discipling ourselves. Staying in fighting shape.

Since churches tend to drift downward into businesses, clubs, police agencies, and cliques, pastors and teachers must always keep the vision before the members.

"We are the family of God, sent to share the good news of Jesus."

Anything less is to violate our assignment.

ABOUT THE AUTHOR

Joe McKeever is a native of Nauvoo, Alabama and lives in the Jackson, Mississippi area. Starting in 1962, he pastored Southern Baptist churches for 42 years, then was director of missions for the SBC churches of New Orleans. He has degrees from Birmingham-Southern College and New Orleans Baptist Theological Seminary.

Joe is the father of two sons and a daughter and grandfather to eight young adults. His wife of 52 years, Margaret, died in January 2015. Two years later, he married Bertha Pepper Fagan, the widow of a pastor friend.

Joe is a cartoonist for Baptist Press (www.bpnews.net) and he blogs regularly at www.joemckeever.com. Among Joe's other books are:

Help! I'm a Deacon

Grief Recovery 101 written with his wife Bertha.

Sixty and Better: Making the Most of Our Golden Years also written with Bertha

Pastoring

Pray Anyway

Listen! God is Speaking

Joe's life-verse is Job 4:4 "Your words have stood men on their feet."

www.ingramcontent.com/pod-product-compliance
Lightning Source LLC
Chambersburg PA
CBHW052159110526
44591CB00012B/2008